STORIES
◆◆ From the Northeast ◆◆

ISBN-13: 978-0-15-352860-6
ISBN-10: 0-15-352860-5

1 2 3 4 5 6 7 8 9 10 179 11 10 09 08 07 06

Harcourt
SCHOOL PUBLISHERS
Visit *The Learning Site!* www.harcourtschool.com

A Land Full of Tales

People love strange and mysterious stories. The Northeast is full of such legends. The area's first storytellers were Native Americans. Later, settlers added their tales. Even now, new legends are being created.

Amazing Places, Amazing Stories

People have always been afraid of Mount Washington, in New Hampshire, and with good reason. At 6,288 feet, it is the Northeast's tallest mountain. The world's strongest recorded wind gust, 231 miles per hour, was measured there in 1934. Native Americans thought the Great Spirit lived at the top. They would never climb to the summit.

Many people believed they saw imaginary people on the mountain. One man heard a party going on, but when he looked, no one else was around. Other people have seen small clouds that looked and moved strangely.

Many people say they have heard or seen strange things near the top of Mount Washington in New Hampshire.

Native Americans told stories about Spirit of Thunder, who lived in Niagara Falls.

Today, visitors can take a boat right up to the falls.

Like Mount Washington, Niagara Falls, New York, is a fascinating place. Hundreds of years ago, Native Americans living in the area knew the falls were special. They told a myth about a snake and a girl there.

In the myth, the girl lets herself fall into the waterfalls to escape the snake. There she meets Spirit of Thunder, who lives in the falls. He catches the falling girl and tells her that a bad spirit is going to send a big water snake to poison her people. Her people must move to a safer spot, farther up the Niagara River. The girl warns her people, and they move to safety. When the snake comes, Spirit of Thunder kills it. As a result, the people are saved and are healthy and happy for many years.

Myths and legends can entertain, tell about people's beliefs, and pass on bits of history. There are often different versions of the same story. Many storytellers work hard to research tales. They make sure they are respectful to people's cultural beliefs and as true to the original stories as possible.

3

Symbols in Stone

Native Americans believed that if they followed a certain river north, they would find a mountain with a stone face. In 1805, a big stone face was found in New Hampshire. People called the rocks the Old Man of the Mountain.

In 1851, Nathaniel Hawthorne wrote a short story called "The Great Stone Face." The story says that someday a great person will be born who looks just like the stone face.

In the story, a boy named Ernest grows up and meets several men who look a little like the Great Stone Face, but Ernest knows that these men are not great. Later, people notice that Ernest looks like the stone face.

Recently, part of the Old Man's "face" fell apart. The face is gone, but people will always remember the monument and its stories.

The Old Man of the Mountain

What's That Noise?

For years, people in Moodus, Connecticut, have been hearing strange noises coming from caves that sound like a train or thunder. The name *Moodus* comes from a Native American word meaning "place of noises." Today, scientists think the noises come from small earthquake activity.

Strange writing at Mystery Hill

Who built the rock caves and tunnels at Mystery Hill, New Hampshire? The answer may never be known.

In Salem, New Hampshire, there is another set of strange rocks. Visitors find stone walls, tunnels, cavelike rooms, and strange picture writing on Mystery Hill.

Some people believe this is a very old place of worship, while a few say Irish monks built it in the tenth century. Others say Native Americans did the building. These rocks, also called "America's Stonehenge," may have been put together more than 4,000 years ago. Like the famous Stonehenge in England, the rocks can be used as a calendar of the sun and moon.

In the 1830s, a farmer owned the land and used some of the caves for storage. These caves may also have been a stop along the Underground Railroad. Escaped slaves heading north to freedom could have hidden there. No matter who built America's Stonehenge, it is an interesting mystery.

5

Tales to Feed Your Imagination

Henry Hudson

Two well-known stories come from the state of New York. Henry Hudson of England is famous for exploring the area's waterways. The Hudson River and Hudson Bay are named after him. A legend says that one night in 1609, near the Catskill Mountains, Hudson heard music. He went ashore with a few members of his crew. They saw gnomes dancing and singing around a fire in the mountains.

According to the legend, the men spent hours talking, dancing, and bowling with the gnomes. When it was time to go, some of Hudson's men had turned into gnomes! Hudson took them back to their ship, where they slept. When they woke, they were back to normal.

Hudson disappeared in 1611, after his ship was frozen in the ice. Legend says that every 20 years, Hudson and his men return to party with the gnomes. People hear music and see fires in the Catskill Mountains. They hear thunder, too, from the bowling.

The Catskill Mountains

A writer named Washington Irving wrote many famous stories about New York. One is called "The Legend of Sleepy Hollow." In the story, a clumsy teacher named Ichabod Crane falls in love with a girl named Katrina. Brom Bones, a handsome troublemaker, also loves Katrina. Both men go to a party at Katrina's house. They eat, dance, and listen to stories. Someone tells of a Headless Horseman who lives in a nearby graveyard.

After the party, Crane must ride his horse home, passing the graveyard. The Headless Horseman chases him. The next morning, Crane cannot be found, although his horse is safe. People look for Crane, but all they find is his hat, a saddle, and a smashed pumpkin. No one ever sees Ichabod Crane again.

Sleepy Hollow Cemetery is a real cemetery in Sleepy Hollow, New York. Washington Irving, who died in 1859, is buried there.

Did the Headless Horseman get Ichabod Crane?

What's Under the Water?

Some people believe a sea monster lives in Lake Champlain, between New York and Vermont. People say "Champ" looks like a snake and is more than 20 feet long. Long ago, Native Americans had a different name for the monster—Tatoskok.

Sandra Mansi says she and her family saw Champ in 1977 and took this picture. Hers is one of the most famous photos of Champ.

In the 1800s, circus founder P. T. Barnum said he would pay $50,000 to anyone who caught the monster, but no one ever did. Recently, people have taken pictures and movies of something in the water.

Scientists have looked for Champ, too. When they listened underwater with microphones, they heard strange noises, like sounds made by a whale or dolphin. Did a sea monster make the noises? No one knows for sure.

And in Lake Memphremagog . . .

Some people believe there is another lake monster in Vermont. This one, called Memphre, is in a lake between Vermont and Canada. More than 200 people believe they have seen this monster in the last 150 years.

Islands in the Connecticut River

People have been looking for Captain Kidd's treasure for years.

One of the most famous stories of the Northeast tells of Captain Kidd's lost treasure. Captain Kidd lived in New York in the late 1600s. King William of England hired him to attack French and Spanish ships. In 1699, however, the British government said Captain Kidd had become a pirate.

Captain Kidd was in the Indian Ocean with a ship full of treasure at the time. When he sailed back to New York, Kidd was arrested and put in jail. He was hanged in 1701 for being a pirate.

Before he was arrested, however, Kidd hid his treasure. It is believed that he buried some on a small island in the Connecticut River. A legend says that only three people digging at midnight under a full moon can find the treasure. The people must form a triangle as they dig, and cannot speak a word. If they break their silence, the treasure will disappear!

Legends from History

Legends are passed down from generation to generation. Some stories don't change much. Other tales are added to, stretched, and sometimes changed completely. The stories of Johnny Appleseed, Uncle Sam, and Mother Goose are examples of legends from history that have stretched and changed.

Johnny and His Apples

Johnny Appleseed's real name was John Chapman. He was born in Massachusetts in 1774. As an adult, he built a cabin in Pennsylvania. There he collected apple seeds from cider mills, planted them, and started orchards. He traveled west and continued to plant orchards all over Ohio and Indiana. Apples were a useful food, and pioneers were glad to buy seeds and trees from Chapman. He was successful at business, but he was generous, too. He traded and gave away apple seeds and trees to settlers who couldn't afford to buy them.

History into Legend

As pioneers carried apple trees west, stories grew about John Chapman. He became more than a careful apple tree grower and an honest and generous man. People talked about how good he was. They said he was always cheerful and that he lived simply. They said he had a long beard, wore old clothes, hardly ever wore shoes, and wore his saucepan on his head for a hat. He could talk to animals, even wolves, and he would sleep in the snow instead of a cave to keep from disturbing a family of bears.

Many of these details come from a magazine article written in 1871. Although no one has proved the truth of these bits of legend, many people believe them. The legend of Johnny Appleseed shows that it isn't always easy to separate real history from a great story.

Johnny Appleseed

History or Legend?

Uncle Sam

People around the world know Uncle Sam as a symbol of the United States. But not everyone knows that the symbol is based on a real person.

Samuel Wilson was born in Massachusetts in 1766. He and his brother started a meat business in New York. Their business did well. People liked the Wilson brothers so much that they called them *Uncle.*

The United States Army started to buy their meat. One day in 1813, someone saw barrels of meat about to be sent to the army and wondered what the letters *US* stood for. Though the letters stood for *United States,* a guard explained that they were Uncle Sam's initials.

People started to say "Uncle Sam" when talking about the U.S. government. Artists drew Uncle Sam in cartoons and, over the years, added a top hat and dressed him in red, white, and blue.

Uncle Sam Wants You!

An artist named James Montgomery Flagg drew one of the most famous pictures of Uncle Sam. Over four million posters were made as the United States entered World War I. The poster said, "I Want You for U.S. Army." The same poster was also used in World War II.

Was Mother Goose Real?

Children around the world know about Jack and Jill and Little Bo Peep. These and other poems are in books by Mother Goose, but was there a real Mother Goose?

Legend says that Mother Goose's real name was Elizabeth Goose and she was buried in Boston, Massachusetts. Elizabeth Mary Goose was a real person. She was born in 1665, but she did not write poems for children. People get confused because after Elizabeth Goose died, one of her relatives wrote an article saying she had written the famous poems.

The fairy tales of *Mother Goose* were actually the work of a French writer in 1696. The book showed a picture of a woman telling stories. In the picture are the words *Tales of My Mother Goose.* People liked that name and kept using it. Rhymes and poems for children made up by many different writers are grouped together and called Mother Goose poems.

Many people who see this Boston grave think it belongs to Mother Goose.

An Old Curse and a Modern Tale

The Curse of the Bambino

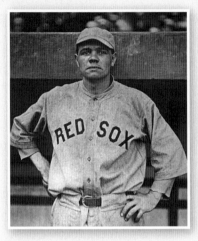

In 1920, the Boston Red Sox sold their star player, Babe Ruth, to the New York Yankees. Ruth was a great player, and he had helped the Red Sox win two World Series. At that time, the Red Sox had won four World Series, more than any other team. After Ruth left, the Red Sox stopped winning the World Series.

George Herman "Babe" Ruth

The Red Sox had years of bad luck. Sportswriters began calling their bad luck the "Curse of the Babe." They also called it the "Curse of the Bambino." They said that the team had been cursed because it traded Babe Ruth to the Yankees. But in 2004, the Red Sox won the World Series!

Finally, after 85 years, the Red Sox won the World Series.

All of the penguins at the New England Aquarium are safe. The story about a stolen penguin is an urban legend.

Urban Legends

Modern tales that sound true but are not are called urban legends. People often tell or e-mail them to one another. They may take place in a metropolitan area, but they don't have to.

One urban legend is about a boy who went on a school trip to the New England Aquarium. He disappeared for a while, and then seemed secretive. Later, at home, his mother found a penguin in the bathtub. The boy had stolen a penguin from the aquarium.

This never happened, although many people are sure it did. For several years, the aquarium got calls about the story. Finally, the aquarium had a press conference. Workers told reporters that the story was made up. All the aquarium's penguins were safe. The reporters realized it would have been impossible for a boy to climb the railing, jump six feet down to the penguin area, and steal the penguin without being seen and stopped!

Think and Respond

1. Who might have built America's Stonehenge?

2. What happens every 20 years in the Catskill Mountains, according to a famous story?

3. Were Johnny Appleseed and Uncle Sam real people? Explain.

4. Why is it hard to tell whether there is a sea monster in Lake Champlain?

5. Why do you think people often believe urban legends like the story about the penguin stolen from the New England Aquarium?

 # Activity

Does your town or region have any myths, stories, or legends based on its history? Find out about one of these special stories. Share it with your classmates by telling it aloud.